by Maria Martinez

Edited by Rick Mattingly

ISBN 978-0-7935-9087-2

HAL•LEONARD®
CORPORATION

7777 W. BLUEMOUND RD. P.O. BOX 13819 MILWAUKEE, WI 53213

Visit Hal Leonard Online at
www.halleonard.com

ACKNOWLEDGMENTS AND DEDICATION

I am grateful to be able to play and teach music as my livelihood, and I owe my gratitude to many special people in my life. I dedicate this book to all those who have helped me realize my goal.

Special thanks to my family for their love and support: Isabel Martinez, Miguel Martinez, Maria and Jorge Gonzalez, Teresa and Bobby Castello, Julie Sulser-Stav and Val Sulser. My deepest thanks to Robin Wright for her companionship, love and endless support of all my endeavors.

Thanks to all my students and teachers for the opportunity to grow and learn. A special thanks to Joe Lambert for being a great teacher and an inspiration. Thanks to all the musicians who have given me the opportunity to pay my rent, play, and grow musically. Special thanks to Lynn Keller, Dennis Beck, and Eddie Roscetti for their friendship and continued support.

Thanks also to all my endorsers for the great equipment and continued support over the years: Paiste, Regal Tip, Latin Percussion, the E-Pad Company, Pearl, Remo Heads, and Rhythm Tech.

Thanks to Jeff Schroedl and Rick Mattingly at Hal Leonard for making this project possible.

CD CREDITS

Drums and Percussion: Maria Martinez; Bass: George Lopez; Keyboards: Cheche Alara; Saxes: Robert Kyle; Trumpet: Ann King. Recorded at The Note Well Studio, Val Verde, California; Engineer: Bob Nagy. Produced by Maria Martinez.

ABOUT THE AUTHOR

Maria Martinez was born in Camaguey, Cuba and raised in New Orleans, Louisiana. She has studied drumset and percussion with Alex Acuna, Steve Houghton, Joe Porcaro, Ralph Humphrey, Joey Baron, Casey Scheuerell, Alan Dawson, and many others.

Martinez is the author of several educational publications, including the *Brazilian Coordination for Drumset* and *Afro-Cuban Coordination for Drumset* books and videos, and *The Instant Guide to Drum Grooves* book/CD packages. She has taught master classes, conducted clinics, and played at events such as PASIC (Percussive Arts Society International Convention), NAMM (National Association of Music Merchants), and TCAP (The California Arts Project), just to name a few.

Martinez pursues an active freelance career, sharing stage and studio with such artists as Barry White, El Chicano, Rita Coolidge, Nel Carter, Angela Bofill, Klymaxx, Emmanuel, Johnny Paycheck, Trini Lopez, and others. Her television and recording appearances include The Late Show, The Drew Carey Show, Dukes of Hazzard, Soul Train, and many others.

CONTENTS

INTRODUCTION

Brazilian Coordination for Drumset will enable you to develop the necessary coordination with which to play in a variety of Brazilian musical styles. By combining ostinatos with a series of progressive coordination studies, the book provides challenging material for drummers at all levels.

Specifically, the book contains in-depth rhythm studies that can be worked out individually with each ostinato in order to develop coordination and rhythmic awareness. These are followed by inclusive summaries that can serve as further coordination studies and as reading exercises.

But *Brazilian Coordination for Drumset* goes beyond just teaching mechanics. The book also contains two-bar rhythmic phrases typical of the Brazilian style that will help you make the transition from practicing coordination exercises to playing music.

The accompanying CD contains demo and play-along tracks in the popular Bossa Nova, Samba, Baiao and Partido Alto styles, which are often played in "Latin jazz" settings. Practicing with the play-along tracks will help you get the feel of the rhythmic style and also help you learn to lock in with other musicians.

In addition to practicing the material in this book, you must listen to the styles of music you intend to learn and play. A selected discography of Brazilian music is included that you can use as a starting point. Listen to the ways in which the drums, percussion, bass, piano, vocals, etc. interact with each other.

Because there are so many ways to play and interpret Brazilian music, I encourage you to check out other Latin drumset books that include Brazilian drumset patterns, percussion parts, and musical history. To learn the "language" of the Brazilian style and its drumming, familiarize yourself with the feel of the music, the traditional percussion instruments used in the music, and the traditional parts played on those instruments.

It is my sincere hope that this book will provide you with an effective and musical way to acquire all the coordination you need in order to express your musical ideas with ease.

Maria Martinez

INTERPRETATION

In order to achieve the proper "feel" for Brazilian music, rhythms must not be played with strict metronomic, mathematical, or "military" subdivisions. Straight eighth and sixteenth notes often have a hint of a swing feel, although not so much as to sound like a shuffle. It's like the way an egg would roll across a table with a sort of "lope" as opposed to the way a tennis ball would roll smoothly.

When playing quarter-note triplets in conjunction with the ostinato patterns in this book, the triplet figures must be loosely interpreted. They are not to be played in a strict three-against-four polyrhythmic manner. The example below illustrates how straight quarter-note triplets on the snare drum would be aligned with a hi-hat/bass drum ostinato in a Bossa Nova or Samba.

But even with the above example, don't play it with a strict interpretation. Put a little bit of "lope" into it. This is why it is very important to listen to a lot of Brazilian music, as the nuances of feel cannot be reflected through notation alone.

GENERAL INSTRUCTIONS

Each ostinato in this book contains a rhythmic pattern played by the feet on hi-hat and bass drum, and most include a ride cymbal or hi-hat part to be played by one hand. Begin by practicing an ostinato as written until you are comfortable with it.

Underneath each Bossa Nova, Samba and Baiao ostinato pattern is a checklist corresponding to Rhythm Studies and Summary pages in Parts I through V. Once you are comfortable with an ostinato, go to the first section indicated in the checklist and learn to play each Rhythm Study along with the ostinato, following the instruction given on each line (e.g., play on snare drum; play with cross-stick technique; play ride cymbal and snare drum in unison). Once you have mastered each of the Rhythm Studies on a page, practice playing the Summary page that follows. At the end of each section there are Comprehensive Summary pages that combine rhythm patterns from Rhythm Studies pages and Summary pages. Once you have completed a section, you can mark it on the checklist and advance to the next section.

For the Partido Alto, 3/4 Bossa Nova/Samba, and 7/4 Bossa Nova/Samba sections, the checklists appear at the bottom of the corresponding Rhythm Studies and Summary pages so that you can keep track of which ostinatos you have mastered with those pages.

It is not necessary to learn the ostinatos in the order in which they are presented in this book. If you wish to skip around, you will find the checklists especially useful in helping you keep track of which patterns you have mastered.

NOTATION KEY

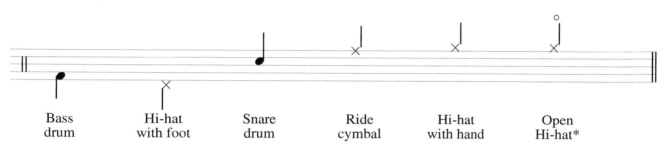

| Bass
drum | Hi-hat
with foot | Snare
drum | Ride
cymbal | Hi-hat
with hand | Open
Hi-hat* |

*Hi-hat should only be opened slightly so as not to interrupt the flow of the pattern.

ADDITIONAL PRACTICE SUGGESTIONS

The purpose of this book is to help you develop the coordination necessary that you can eventually improvise freely on the snare drum while maintaining an ostinato with the other three limbs. One way to begin to develop that ability is to play each two-bar phrase in Part V, and then "answer" that phrase with an improvised phrase of your own. You could also play two consecutive two-bar phrases from Part V and then improvise a four-bar phrase, thereby "trading fours" with yourself.

On ostinato patterns written only for the feet, in which the instruction is to play the rhythms in the Rhythm Studies and Summary pages hand-to-hand, you could also incorporate tom-toms as a way of developing fill and solo patterns that can be played while maintaining an ostinato with the feet.

CD TRACKS

In order to assist you in developing the proper "feel" for the Brazilian rhythms covered in this book, the accompanying compact disc features demonstration and play-along tracks that can be used when practicing the ostinatos along with the Coordination Patterns and Summary pages, as well as to practice improvising on the snare drum while maintaining an ostinato.

All the tracks on this CD are played in 8-bar phrases. A demonstration is followed by a play-along. The length of each play-along is indicated by how many 8-bar phrases are repeated (e.g., 6X means 8 bars of music is repeated 6 times).

1   Bossa Nova demonstration (ostinato 1, p 9)

2   Bossa Nova play-along (8X, quarter note = 116)

3   Bossa Nova demonstration (ostinato 2, p 9)

4   Bossa Nova play-along (10X, quarter note = 152)

5   Samba demonstration (ostinato 12, p 12)

6   Samba play-along (10X, half note = 80)

7   Samba demonstration (ostinato 3, p 10)

8   Samba play-along (12X, half note = 100)

9   Samba demonstration (ostinato 4, p 10)

10   Samba play-along (16X, half note = 120)

11   Baiao demonstration (ostinato 9, p 14)

12   Baiao play-along (16X, half note = 100)

13   Baiao demonstration (ostinato 3, p 13)

14   Baiao play-along (12X, half note = 116)

15   Baiao demonstration (ostinato 7, p 14)

16   Baiao play-along (16X, half note = 120)

17   Partido Alto demonstration (ostinato 6, p 61)

18   Partido Alto play-along (16X, half note = 100)

19   Partido Alto demonstration (ostinato 8, p 61)

20   Partido Alto play-along (12X, half note = 116)

21   Partido Alto demonstration (ostinato 7, p 61)

22   Partido Alto play-along (16X, half note = 120)

The following demonstrations and play-alongs alternate the two styles in 8-bar phrases 1X each.

23   Partido Alto/Bossa Nova demonstration (ostinato 2, p 61; ostinato 1, p 9)

24   Partido Alto/Bossa Nova play-along (9X, quarter note = 152)

25   Partido Alto/Samba demonstration (ostinato 3, p 61; ostinato 3, p 10)

26   Partido Alto/Samba play-along (12X, half note = 100)

27   Partido Alto/Samba demonstration (ostinato 4, p 61; ostinato 2, p 10)

28   Partido Alto/Samba play-along (9X, half note = 126)

29   3/4 Bossa Nova demonstration (ostinato 5, p 64)

30   3/4 Bossa Nova play-along (6X, quarter note = 68)

31   3/4 Samba demonstration (ostinato 2, p 64)

Note: The conceptual approach for playing Samba and Baiao on the snare drum is mostly improvisational. In some musical situations playing a repetitive rhythmic phrase is a more appropriate approach. The playing of ghost notes with occasional accents and/or press rolls with an improvisational approach are demonstrated on tracks 7, 9, 13, 15, 27, 33, 35, 41 and 47.

Ostinatos that are demonstrated on the CD are identified with the corresponding track number inside a black diamond next to the written example.

DISCOGRAPHY

Listening to Brazilian music is extremely important in developing your ability to improvise in these musical styles. The following Discography is provided to help you locate recordings featuring the styles covered in this book.

O Samba, Brazil Classics 2, Warner Bros. 26019-2. A great collection of popular Samba singers and recordings compiled by David Byrne.

Sergio Mendes, *Oceano*, Verve Forecast 314 532 441-2. Contemporary Brazilian music.

Kevyn Lettau, *Simple Life*, JVC 2016-2. Contemporary Brazilian music.

Brazilliance: The Music Of Rhythm, RCD 20153. A compilation of great Samba singer/composers.

Sambas de Enredo, Carnaval 89 Gravaacoes originais: *Das Escolas De Samba Do Grupo* 1A, RCA Kaiser (LP) 122.00002 & MC 772.00002. A compilation of songs from the top samba schools.

Tania Maria, *Piquant*, Concord Jazz CJP-151. Contemporary Brazilian music.

Brazil Classics 3, Forro, Warner Bros. 926323-2. A collection of music from the Northeast of Brazil, called Forro, compiled by Daved Byrne. Cajun-like folk music using vocals, accordion and percussion.

Antonio Carlos Jobim, *Passarim*, Verve Records 4228 332341. Bossa Nova.

Joao Gilberto, *The Legendary Joao Gilberto*, The Original Bossa Nova Recordings
(1958-1961) World Pacific B4 93891.

Martinho Da Villa, *Canta Canta, Minha Gente*, RCA Victor 110.0002.

Ivan Lins, *Ivan Lins, A Noite*, EMO 064-422849.

Gal Costa, *Cantar*, Philips 6349.117

Milton Nascimento, *Clube Da Esquina*, EMI 664.791606-02

BOSSA NOVA OSTINATOS

The Bossa Nova ostinatos are written in 4/4 (common time), which is how that rhythm is typically thought of and notated. Therefore, concentrate on the quarter-note pulse when working with these patterns. All of the rhythm studies and summary pages, however, are written in cut time, which is how the Samba and Baiao rhythms are felt. The rhythm studies and summary pages should be interpreted as 4/4 when played in conjunction with the Bossa Nova. Ostinatos 1 and 3 may be played by slightly accenting the ride cymbal or hi-hat in unison with the snare drum or cross-stick rhythms.

The rolls in Part V should be played as press rolls with one stick when playing the Bossa Nova ostinatos. The half notes written in the bass drum position in Part V indicate the surdo pulse that is part of the samba feel. Ignore these notes when using Part V with the Bossa Nova ostinatos.

Tempo range: ♩ = 116–152

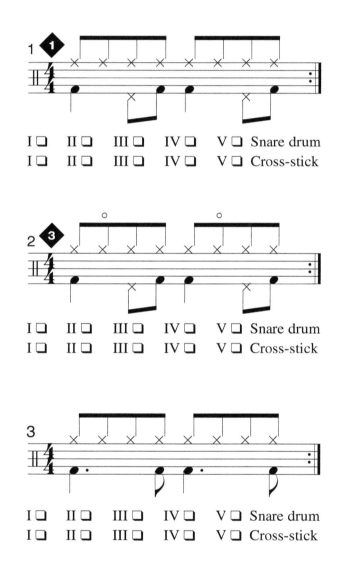

1 I ❏ II ❏ III ❏ IV ❏ V ❏ Snare drum
   I ❏ II ❏ III ❏ IV ❏ V ❏ Cross-stick

2 I ❏ II ❏ III ❏ IV ❏ V ❏ Snare drum
   I ❏ II ❏ III ❏ IV ❏ V ❏ Cross-stick

3 I ❏ II ❏ III ❏ IV ❏ V ❏ Snare drum
   I ❏ II ❏ III ❏ IV ❏ V ❏ Cross-stick

SAMBA OSTINATOS

amba is often written in 4/4 time, but is correctly felt and played with a "two" feel, and so the ostinatos are notated here in cut time. The bass drum part written in the Samba ostinatos emulates the surdo part and should be accented on beat 2. But this should not be a heavy accent; rather, the beat should simply be stressed. Follow the general instructions given in the Introduction section of the book.

The Summary pages in Part V should be played as written on the snare drum, played again on the snare drum with the press rolls omitted, and then played with cross-stick technique (omitting the press rolls).

The half notes written in the bass drum position in Part V represent the surdo drum part, which is an important element of the Samba style. The surdo is a large, low-pitched drum that maintains the underlying pulse of Samba. The cross (+) below the half note indicates a muted stroke; the circle (°) is an accented open tone. For further practice, you can play the notated surdo part in Part V with the right hand on a floor tom with a timpani mallet, while playing the snare drum rhythms with the left hand.

Tempo range: ♩ = 80–120

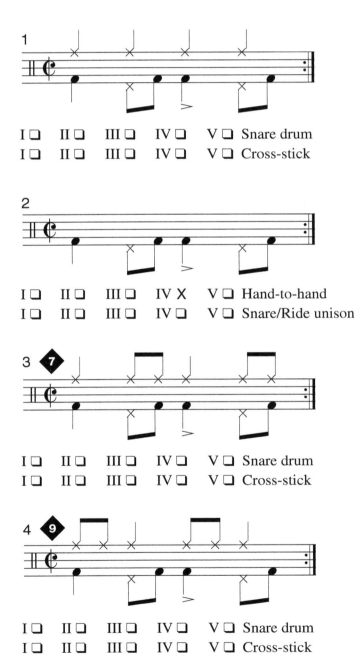

1
I ❑ II ❑ III ❑ IV ❑ V ❑ Snare drum
I ❑ II ❑ III ❑ IV ❑ V ❑ Cross-stick

2
I ❑ II ❑ III ❑ IV X V ❑ Hand-to-hand
I ❑ II ❑ III ❑ IV ❑ V ❑ Snare/Ride unison

3
I ❑ II ❑ III ❑ IV ❑ V ❑ Snare drum
I ❑ II ❑ III ❑ IV ❑ V ❑ Cross-stick

4
I ❑ II ❑ III ❑ IV ❑ V ❑ Snare drum
I ❑ II ❑ III ❑ IV ❑ V ❑ Cross-stick

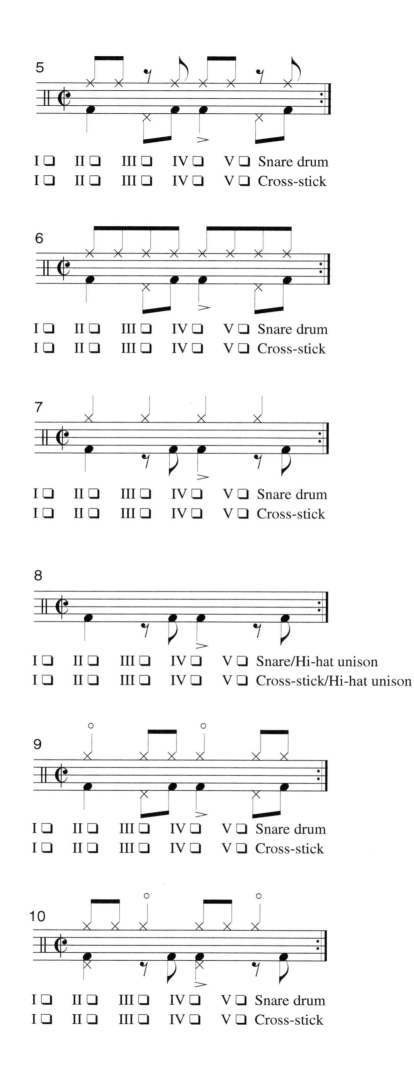

5

I ☐   II ☐   III ☐   IV ☐   V ☐ Snare drum
I ☐   II ☐   III ☐   IV ☐   V ☐ Cross-stick

6

I ☐   II ☐   III ☐   IV ☐   V ☐ Snare drum
I ☐   II ☐   III ☐   IV ☐   V ☐ Cross-stick

7

I ☐   II ☐   III ☐   IV ☐   V ☐ Snare drum
I ☐   II ☐   III ☐   IV ☐   V ☐ Cross-stick

8

I ☐   II ☐   III ☐   IV ☐   V ☐ Snare/Hi-hat unison
I ☐   II ☐   III ☐   IV ☐   V ☐ Cross-stick/Hi-hat unison

9

I ☐   II ☐   III ☐   IV ☐   V ☐ Snare drum
I ☐   II ☐   III ☐   IV ☐   V ☐ Cross-stick

10

I ☐   II ☐   III ☐   IV ☐   V ☐ Snare drum
I ☐   II ☐   III ☐   IV ☐   V ☐ Cross-stick

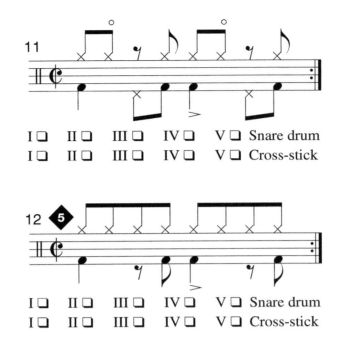

11

I ❑   II ❑   III ❑   IV ❑   V ❑   Snare drum
I ❑   II ❑   III ❑   IV ❑   V ❑   Cross-stick

12

I ❑   II ❑   III ❑   IV ❑   V ❑   Snare drum
I ❑   II ❑   III ❑   IV ❑   V ❑   Cross-stick

BAIAO OSTINATOS

Although Baiao and Samba have different underlying pulses, they are both felt and played with a "two" feel, and so the Baiao ostinatos are notated in cut-time. The bass drum in these ostinatos emulates the rhythm played by the zabumba, a type of surdo drum used in the Baiao musical style. Be sure to accent the bass drum slightly on the "and" of two, as indicated.

Follow the general instructions given in the Introduction section of the book. When practicing the summary pages in Part V, first play them as written, playing the rolls as press rolls with one stick. Then play them again but omit the rolls, and finally play them with the cross-stick technique. The half notes written in the bass drum position in Part V indicate the surdo pulse that is part of the samba feel. Ignore these notes when using Part V with the Baiao ostinatos.

Tempo range: ♩ = 100–120

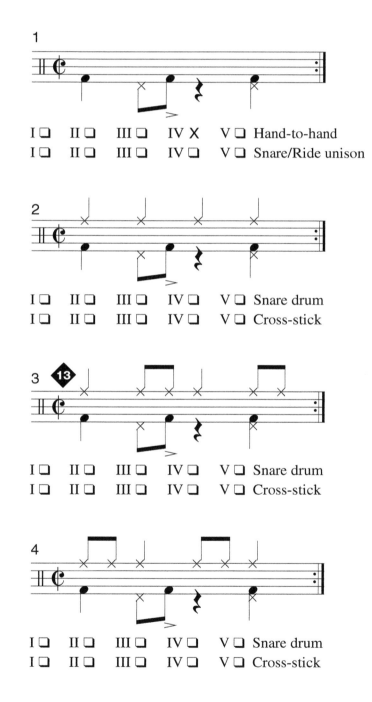

1

I ❑ II ❑ III ❑ IV X V ❑ Hand-to-hand
I ❑ II ❑ III ❑ IV ❑ V ❑ Snare/Ride unison

2

I ❑ II ❑ III ❑ IV ❑ V ❑ Snare drum
I ❑ II ❑ III ❑ IV ❑ V ❑ Cross-stick

3

I ❑ II ❑ III ❑ IV ❑ V ❑ Snare drum
I ❑ II ❑ III ❑ IV ❑ V ❑ Cross-stick

4

I ❑ II ❑ III ❑ IV ❑ V ❑ Snare drum
I ❑ II ❑ III ❑ IV ❑ V ❑ Cross-stick

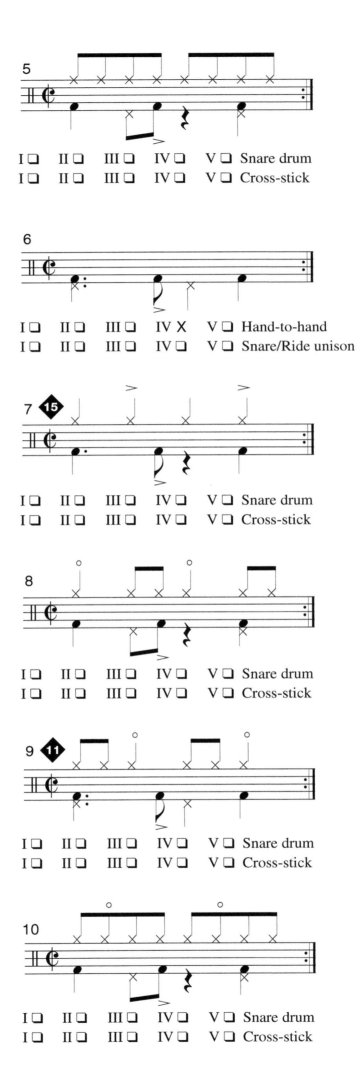

5

I ☐ II ☐ III ☐ IV ☐ V ☐ Snare drum
I ☐ II ☐ III ☐ IV ☐ V ☐ Cross-stick

6

I ☐ II ☐ III ☐ IV X V ☐ Hand-to-hand
I ☐ II ☐ III ☐ IV ☐ V ☐ Snare/Ride unison

7 ◆15

I ☐ II ☐ III ☐ IV ☐ V ☐ Snare drum
I ☐ II ☐ III ☐ IV ☐ V ☐ Cross-stick

8

I ☐ II ☐ III ☐ IV ☐ V ☐ Snare drum
I ☐ II ☐ III ☐ IV ☐ V ☐ Cross-stick

9 ◆11

I ☐ II ☐ III ☐ IV ☐ V ☐ Snare drum
I ☐ II ☐ III ☐ IV ☐ V ☐ Cross-stick

10

I ☐ II ☐ III ☐ IV ☐ V ☐ Snare drum
I ☐ II ☐ III ☐ IV ☐ V ☐ Cross-stick

PART I: RHYTHM STUDIES

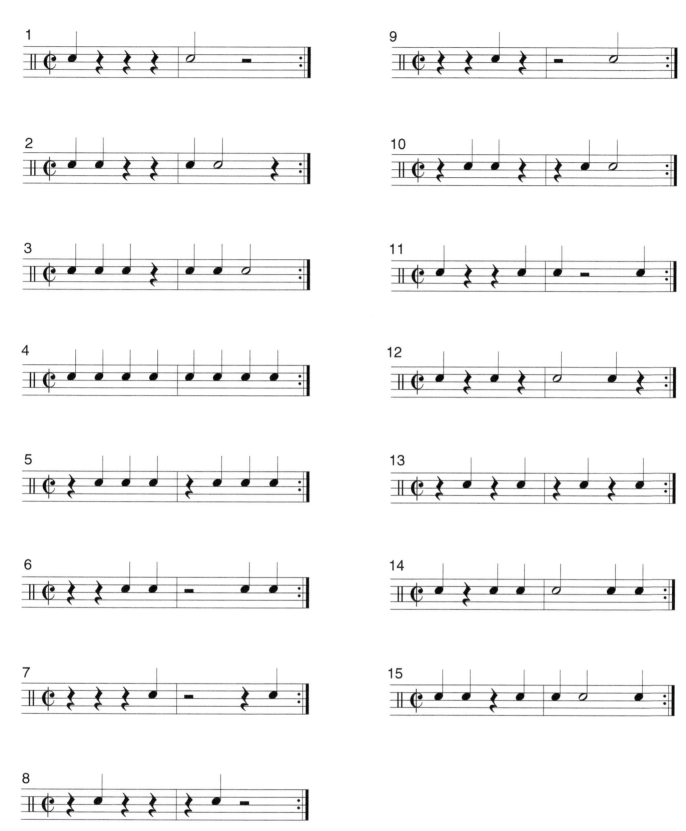

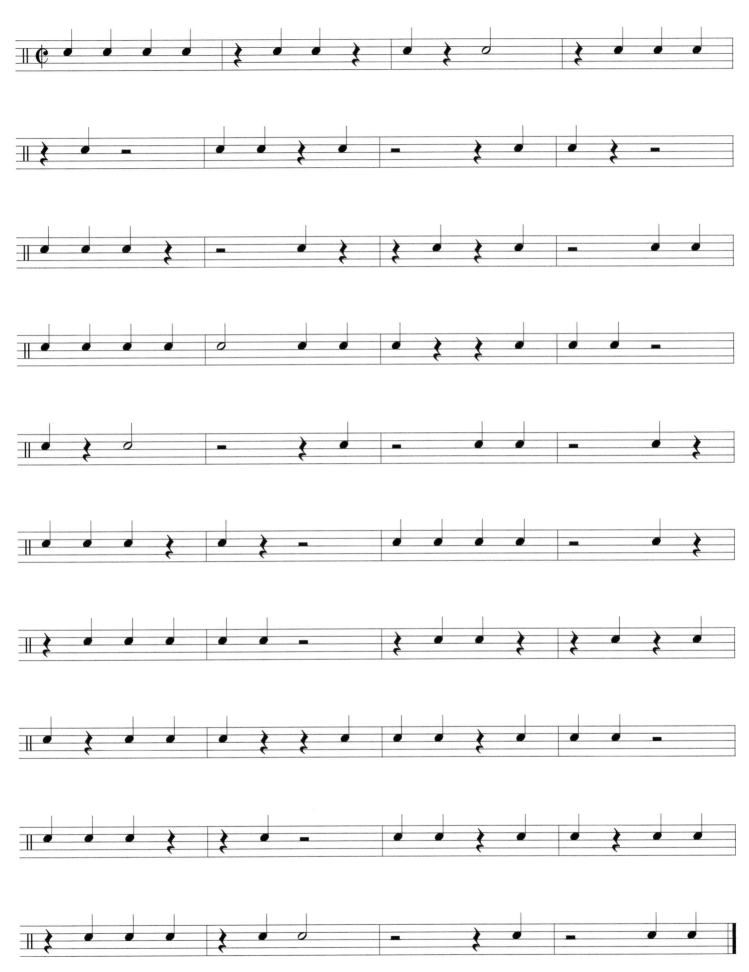

PART II: RHYTHM STUDIES

PART II: RHYTHM STUDIES, continued

PART III: RHYTHM STUDIES

PART III: SUMMARY FROM RHYTHM STUDIES 1-20

PART III: RHTYHM STUDIES, continued

PART III: RHYTHM STUDIES, continued

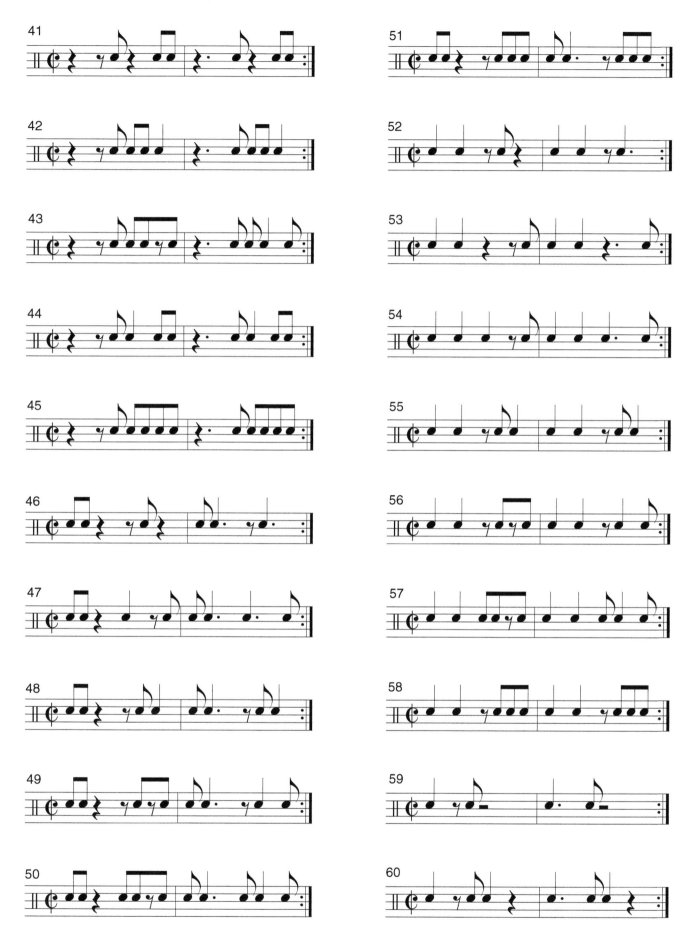

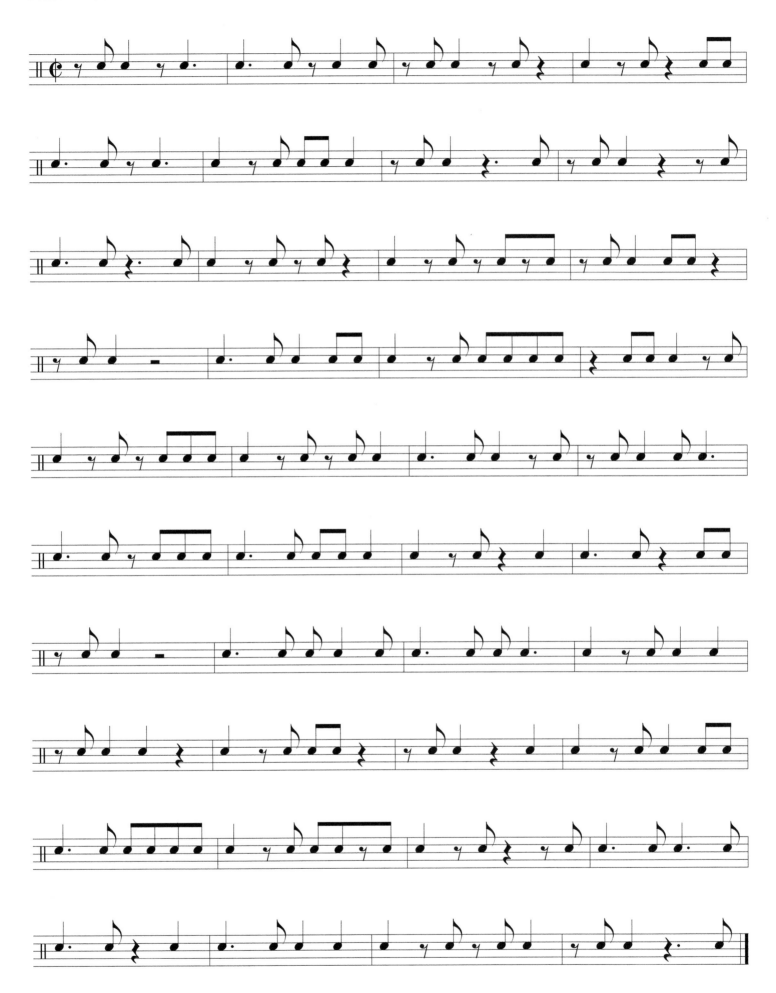

PART III: RHTYHM STUDIES, continued

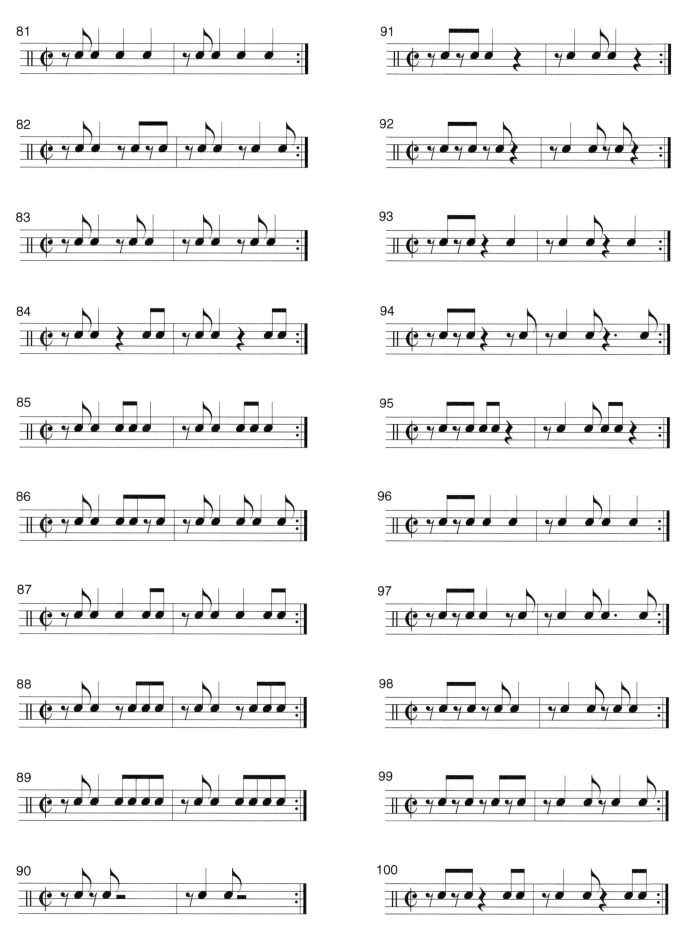

PART III: SUMMARY FROM RHYTHM STUDIES 81-100

PART III: RHTYHM STUDIES, continued

PART III: RHYTHM STUDIES, continued

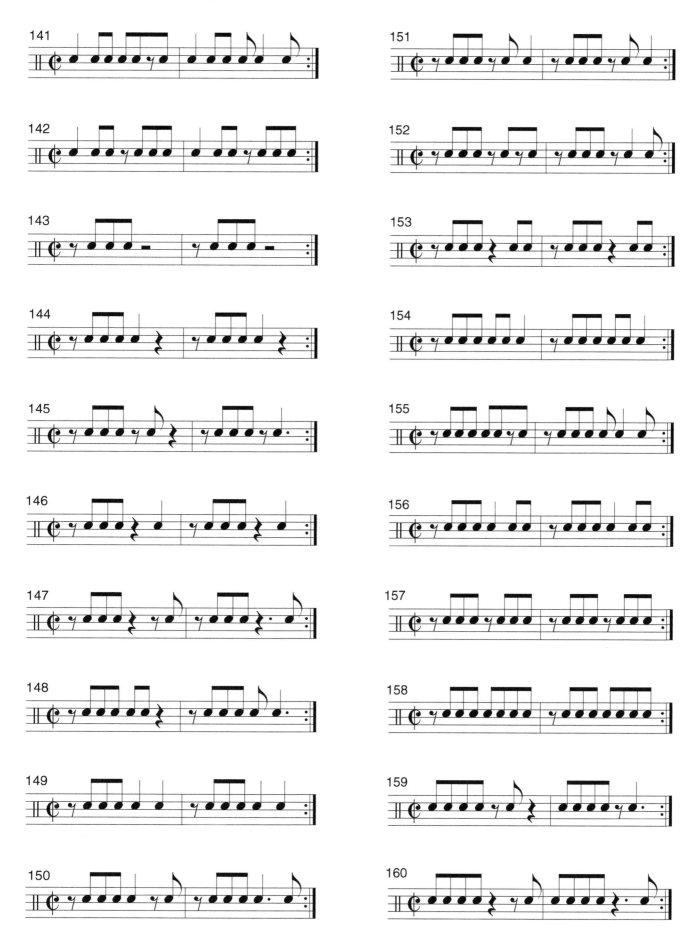

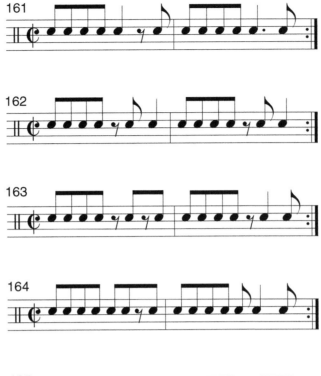

PART III: SUMMARY FROM RHYTHM STUDIES 141-165

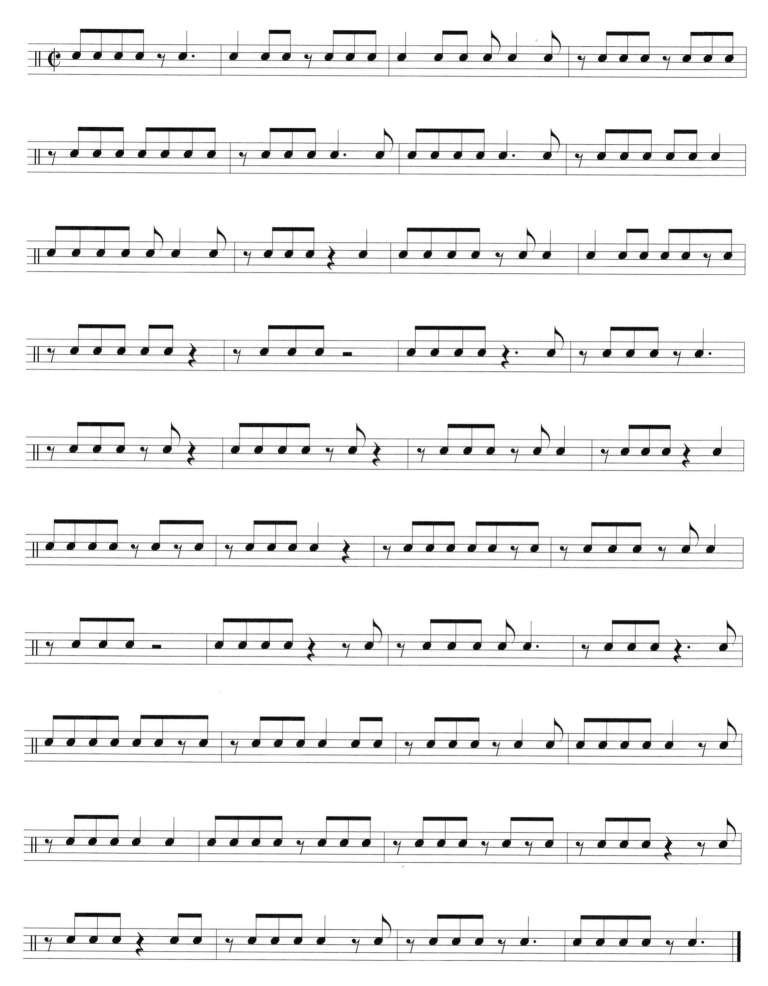

PART III: SUMMARY B FROM PARTS I-III

PART IV: RHYTHM STUDIES

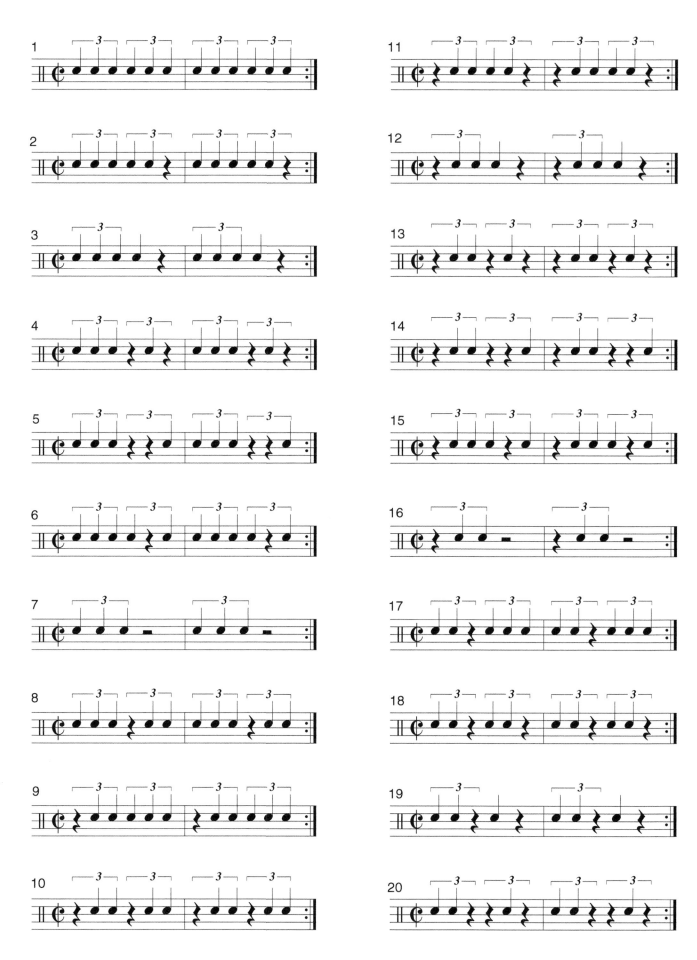

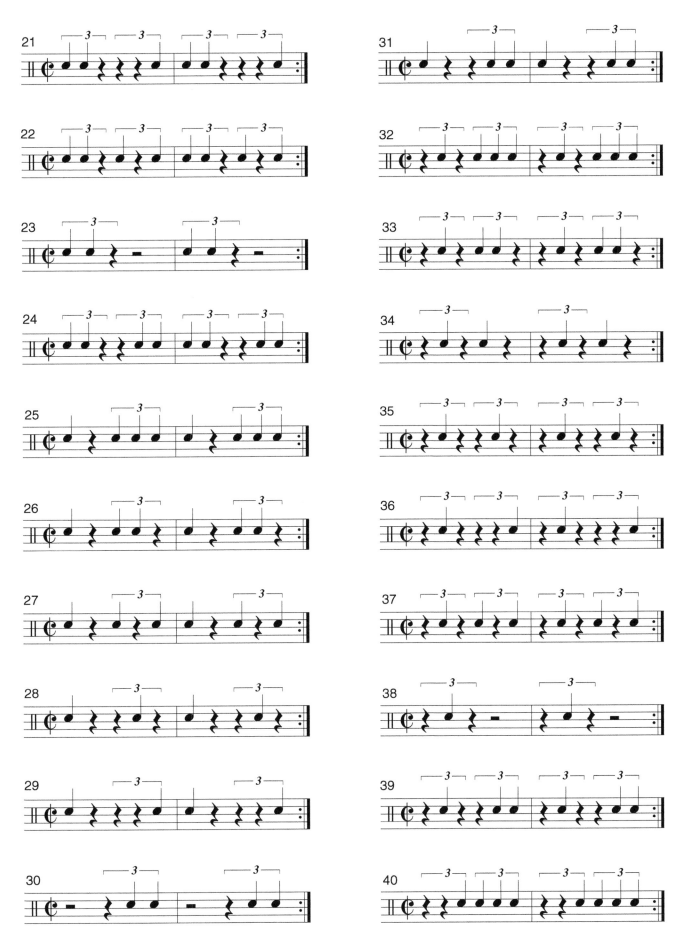

PART IV: SUMMARY FROM RHYTHM STUDIES 1-40

PART IV: RHYTHM STUDIES, continued

PART IV: SUMMARY A FROM RHYTHM STUDIES 1-60

PART IV: SUMMARY B FROM RHYTHM STUDIES 1-60

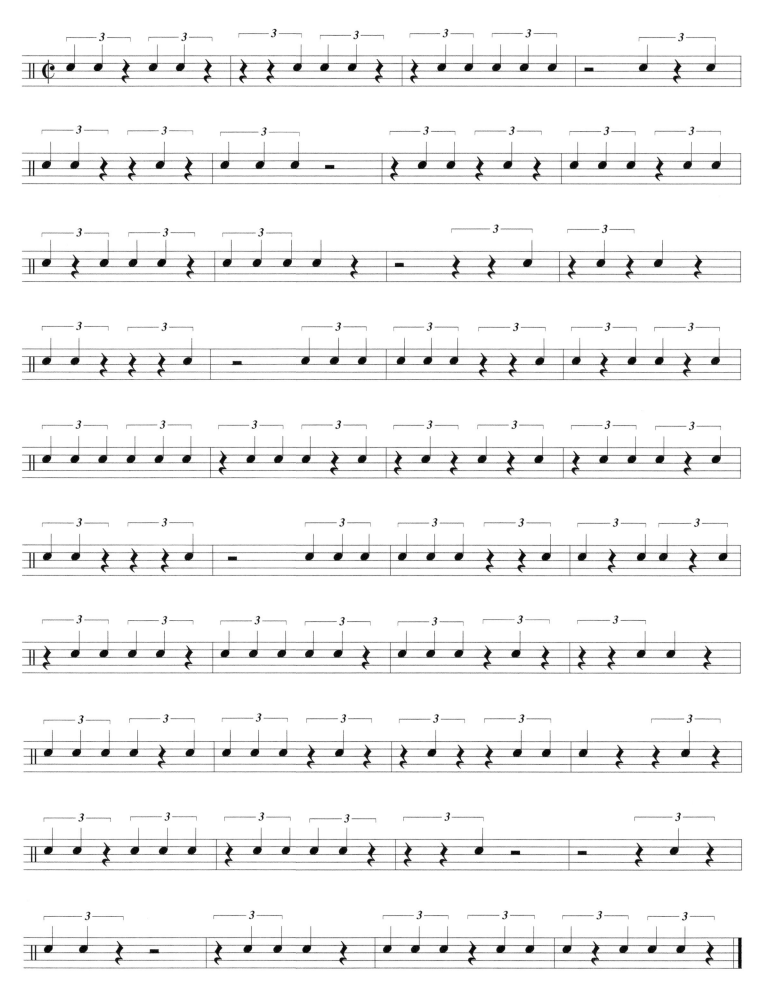

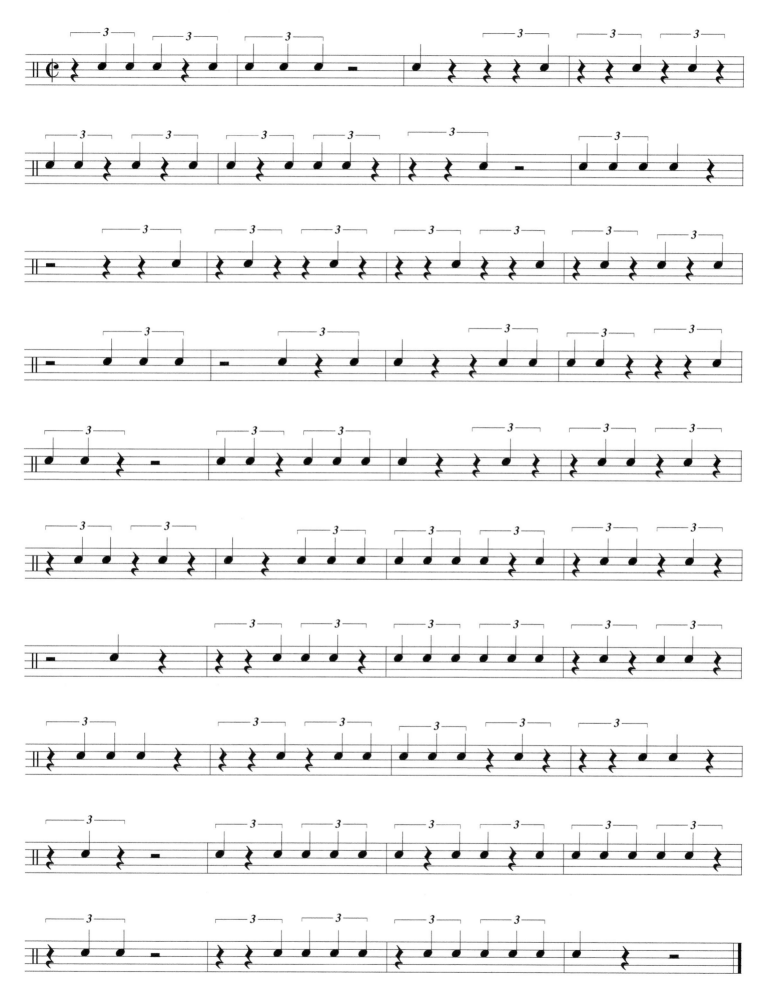

PART IV: SUMMARY D FROM RHYTHM STUDIES 1-60

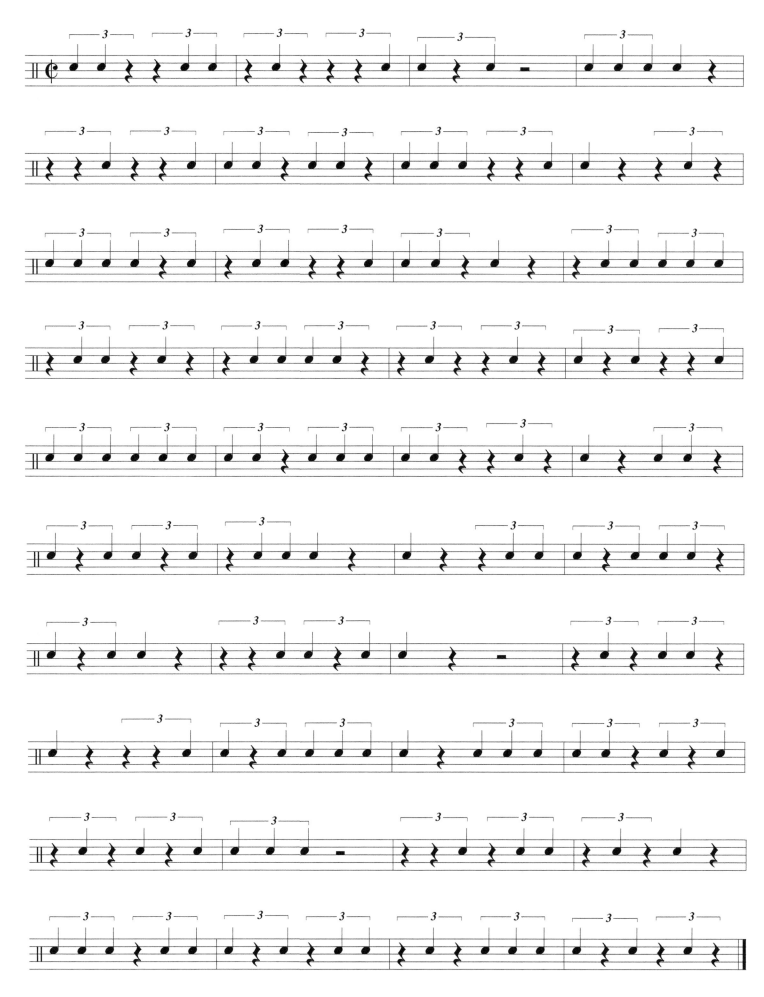

PART IV: SUMMARY B FROM PARTS I-IV

PART IV: SUMMARY C FROM PARTS I-IV

PART V: RHYTHM STUDIES

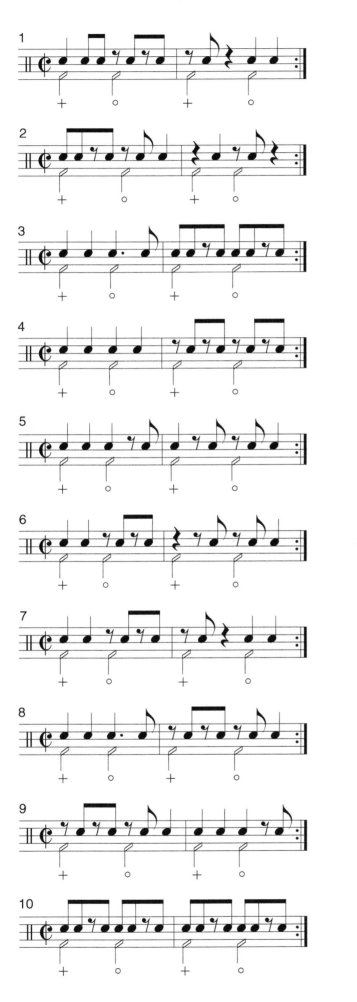

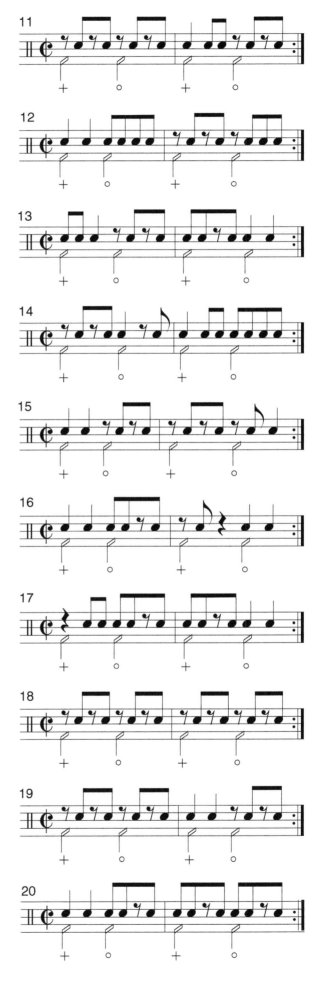

PART V: RHYTHM STUDIES, continued

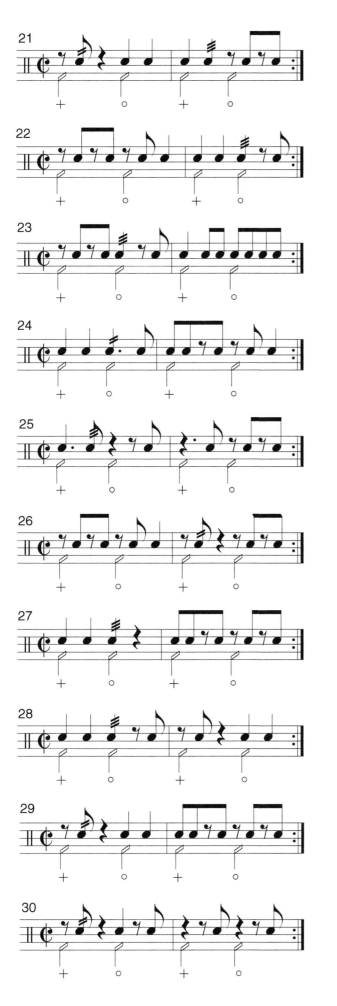
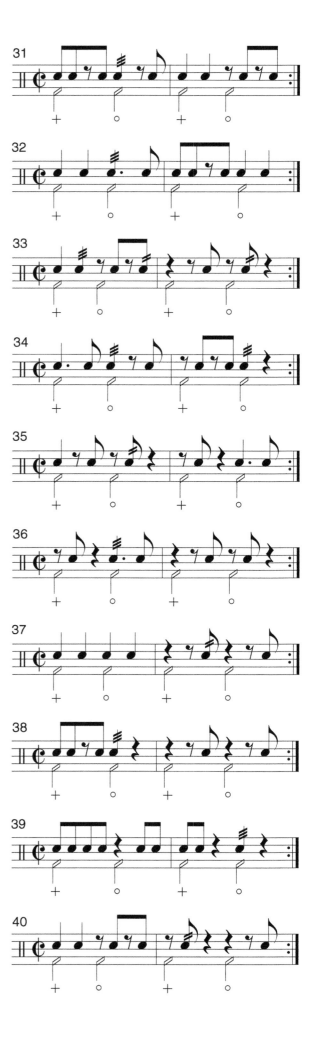

PART V: SUMMARY A

PART V: SUMMARY B

PART V: SUMMARY C

PARTIDO ALTO OSTINATOS

The Partido Alto is a very "hip" style of Samba sometimes referred to as Funk Samba. The Partido Alto groove is often played during a section (e.g., intro, bridge) of a Bossa Nova or Samba.

In this section, the ostinatos consist only of ride cymbal or hi-hat patterns. The Partido Alto exercises that follow consist of two-bar bass drum/snare drum phrases. Practice each of these phrases with all of the Partido Alto ostinatos, using regular snare drum strokes as well as cross-stick technique. Each of the two-bar exercises begins with a pick-up bar. Begin by counting one bar of half notes, then play the pick-up bar, then play the two-bar phrase at least twice before moving to the next exercise.

Once you are comfortable playing the Partido Alto, play eight bars of a Bossa Nova groove, then play eight bars of the Partido Alto, and continue going back and forth between the two grooves. (When playing the Partido Alto in conjunction with the Bossa Nova, think of the Partido Alto in 4/4 rather than in cut-time.) You can also alternate eight bars of Partido Alto with eight bars of Samba. CD tracks 23–28 contain demonstrations and play-alongs of this concept. Note: Partido Alto Rhythmic Phrases 1–10 will sound best with the Partido Alto play-along tracks on the CD, due to the specific rhythm played by the piano on these tracks.

Ostinatos 2 and 6 are appropriate for slow to medium tempos; ostinatos 1, 3, 4, 5, 8 and 9 are appropriate for medium to fast tempos. Ostinato 7 can be used for fast tempos by substituting snare drum notes with either hand.

Tempo range: ♩ = 76–120

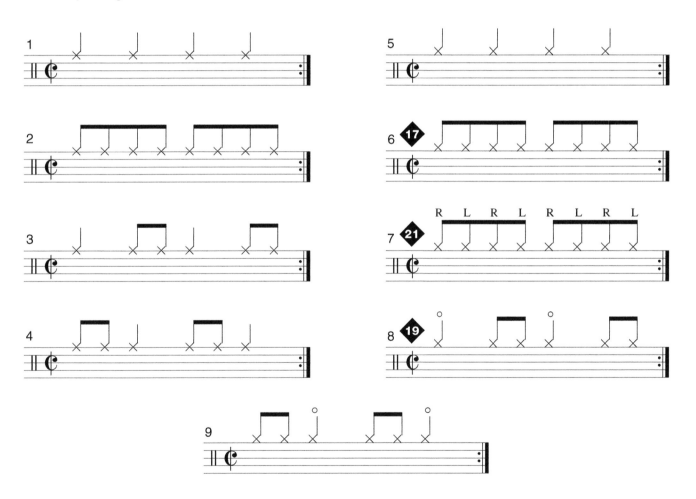

PARTIDO ALTO RHYTHMIC PHRASES

Partido Alto Ostinatos: 1 ☐   2 ☐   3 ☐   4 ☐   5 ☐   6 ☐   7 ☐   8 ☐   9 ☐

3/4 SAMBA/BOSSA NOVA OSTINATOS

Below are five ostinato patterns that can be used for playing Sambas and Bossa Novas in 3/4 time. On the following pages are two-bar Brazilian rhythmic phrases and summaries in 3/4 time that can be practiced with the ostinatos to develop coordination between the snare drum, bass drum, and ride cymbal/hi-hat.

When using the rhythmic phrases and summaries with ostinato 1, play all of the rhythms in unison on the snare drum and ride cymbal, and also play the rhythms hand-to-hand on the snare drum. With ostinatos 2–5, play all exercises on the snare drum, and also play them using cross-stick technique, omitting the press rolls.

Tempo range: ♩ = 68–122

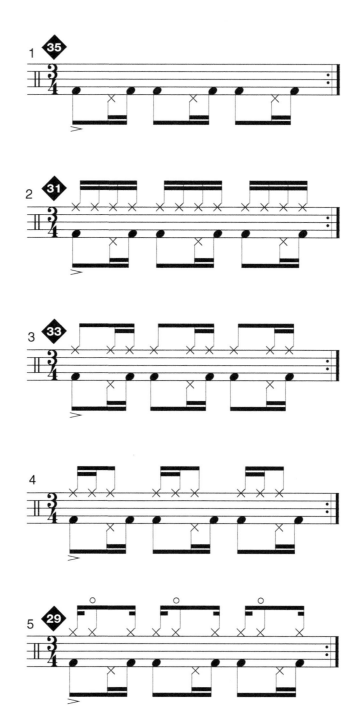

3/4 RHYTHM STUDIES

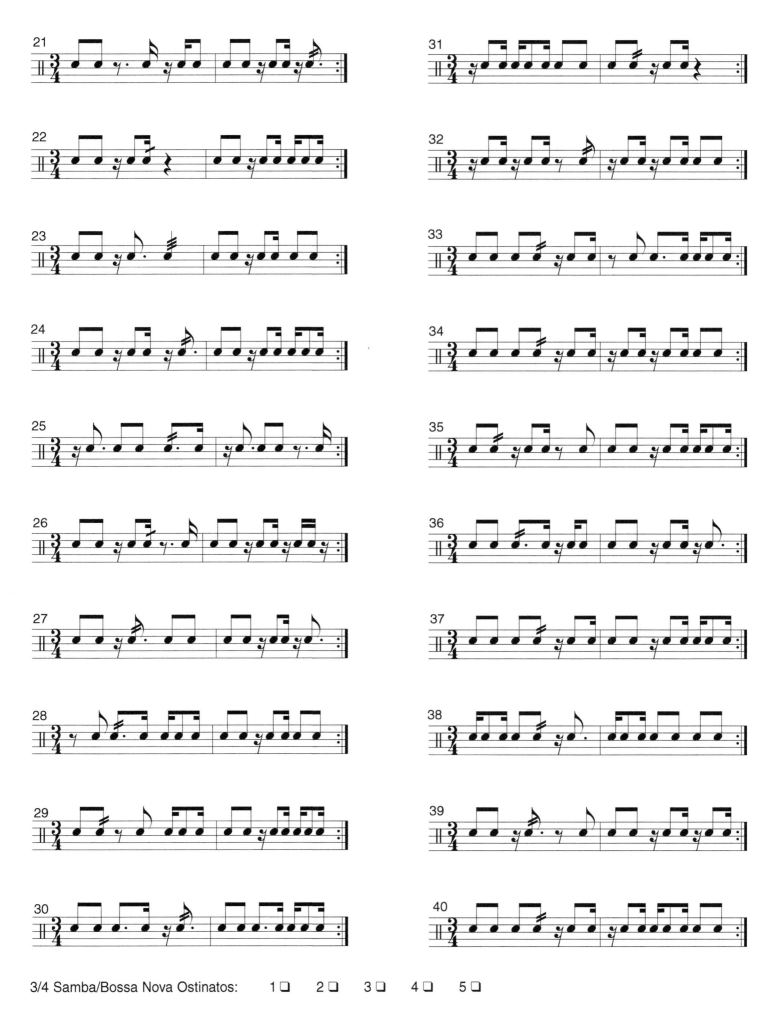

3/4 Samba/Bossa Nova Ostinatos: 1□   2□   3□   4□   5□

3/4 SUMMARY A

3/4 Samba/Bossa Nova Ostinatos: 1☐   2☐   3☐   4☐   5☐

3/4 SUMMARY B

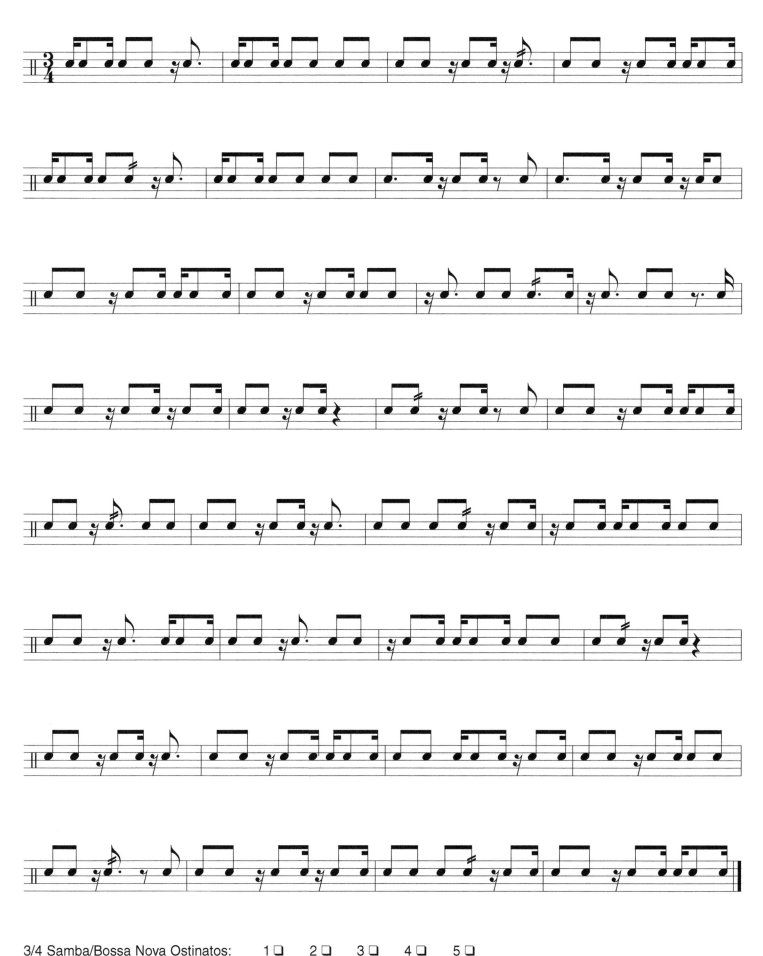

3/4 Samba/Bossa Nova Ostinatos: 1☐ 2☐ 3☐ 4☐ 5☐

3/4 SUMMARY C

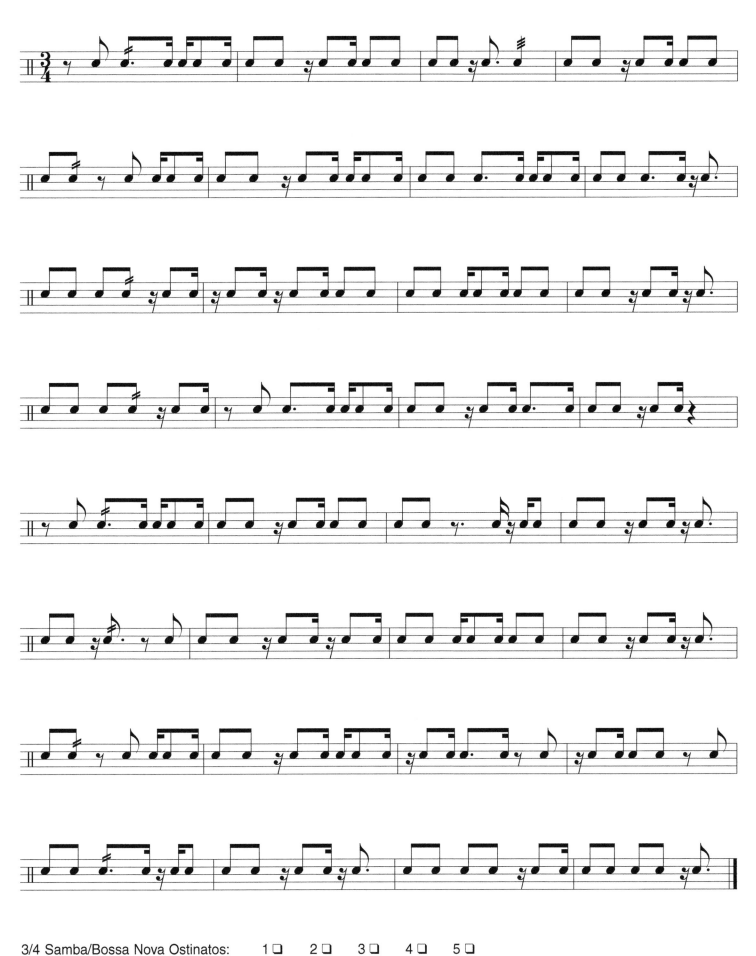

3/4 Samba/Bossa Nova Ostinatos: 1 ☐   2 ☐   3 ☐   4 ☐   5 ☐

3/4 SUMMARY D

3/4 Samba/Bossa Nova Ostinatos: 1☐   2☐   3☐   4☐   5☐

7/4 SAMBA/BOSSA NOVA OSTINATOS

The ostinato patterns in this section can be used for playing Sambas and Bossa Novas in 7/4 time. Following the ostinatos are forty Brazilian rhythmic phrases and four summary pages in 7/4 time that can be practiced with the ostinatos to develop coordination between the snare drum, bass drum, and ride cymbal/hi-hat.

When using the rhythmic phrases and summaries with ostinato 1, play all of the rhythms in unison on the snare drum and ride cymbal, and also play the rhythms hand-to-hand on the snare drum. With ostinatos 2–17, play all exercises on the snare drum, and also play them using cross-stick technique, omitting the press rolls.

Tempo range: ♩ = 130–220

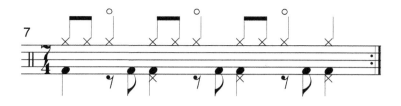

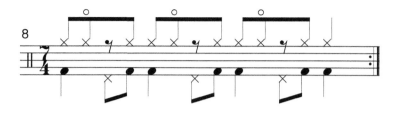

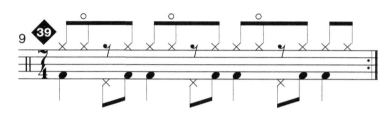

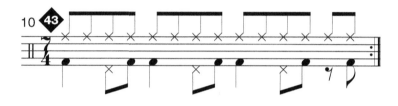

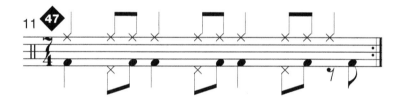

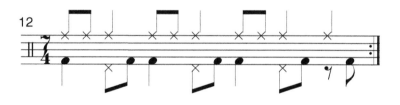

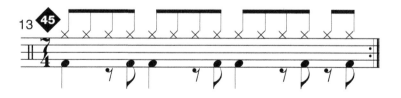

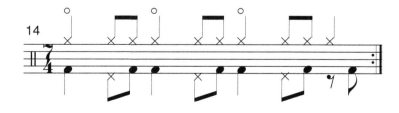

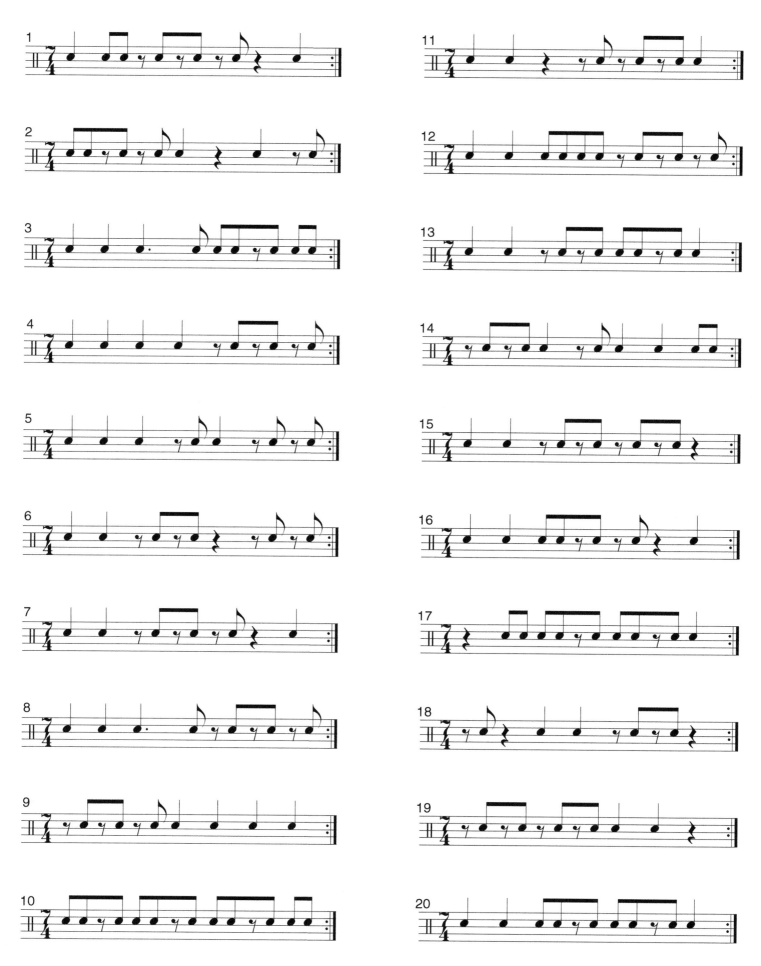

7/4 RHYTHM STUDIES, continued

7/4 Samba/Bossa Nova Ostinatos: 1 ❑   2 ❑   3 ❑   4 ❑   5 ❑   6 ❑   7 ❑   8 ❑   9 ❑
10 ❑   11 ❑   12 ❑   13 ❑   14 ❑   15 ❑   16 ❑   17 ❑

7/4 SUMMARY A

7/4 Samba/Bossa Nova Ostinatos: 1❑ 2❑ 3❑ 4❑ 5❑ 6❑ 7❑ 8❑ 9❑
10❑ 11❑ 12❑ 13❑ 14❑ 15❑ 16❑ 17❑

7/4 SUMMARY B

7/4 Samba/Bossa Nova Ostinatos: 1 ❑   2 ❑   3 ❑   4 ❑   5 ❑   6 ❑   7 ❑   8 ❑   9 ❑

10 ❑   11 ❑   12 ❑   13 ❑   14 ❑   15 ❑   16 ❑   17 ❑

7/4 Samba/Bossa Nova Ostinatos: 1☐ 2☐ 3☐ 4☐ 5☐ 6☐ 7☐ 8☐ 9☐
10☐ 11☐ 12☐ 13☐ 14☐ 15☐ 16☐ 17☐

MUSICIANS INSTITUTE PRESS is the official series of Southern California's renowned music school, Musicians Institute. MI instructors, some of the finest musicians in the world, share their vast knowledge and experience with you – no matter what your current level. For guitar, bass, drums, vocals, and keyboards, MI Press offers the finest music curriculum for higher learning through a variety of series:

ESSENTIAL CONCEPTS	MASTER CLASS	PRIVATE LESSONS
Designed from MI core curriculum programs.	*Designed from MI elective courses.*	*Tackle a variety of topics "one-on one" with MI faculty instructors.*

GUITAR

Acoustic Artistry
by Evan Hirschelman • **Private Lessons**
00695922 Book/Online Audio $19.99

Advanced Scale Concepts & Licks for Guitar
by Jean Marc Belkadi • **Private Lessons**
00695298 Book/CD Pack $19.99

All-in-One Guitar Soloing Course
by Daniel Gilbert & Beth Marlis
00217709 Book/Online Media $29.99

Blues/Rock Soloing for Guitar
by Robert Calva • **Private Lessons**
00695680 Book/CD Pack $19.99

Blues Guitar Soloing
by Keith Wyatt • **Master Class**
00695132 Book/Online Audio $29.99

Blues Rhythm Guitar
by Keith Wyatt • **Master Class**
00695131 Book/Online Audio $19.99

Dean Brown
00696002 DVD $29.95

Chord Progressions for Guitar
by Tom Kolb • **Private Lessons**
00695664 Book/Online Audio $19.99

Chord Tone Soloing
by Barrett Tagliarino • **Private Lessons**
00695855 Book/Online Audio $24.99

Chord-Melody Guitar
by Bruce Buckingham • **Private Lessons**
00695646 Book/Online Audio $19.99

Classical & Fingerstyle Guitar Techniques
by David Oakes • **Master Class**
00695171 Book/Online Audio $19.99

Classical Themes for Electric Guitar
by Jean Marc Belkadi • **Private Lessons**
00695806 Book/CD Pack $15.99

Country Guitar
by Al Bonhomme • **Master Class**
00695661 Book/Online Audio $19.99

Diminished Scale for Guitar
by Jean Marc Belkadi • **Private Lessons**
00695227 Book/CD Pack $14.99

Essential Rhythm Guitar
by Steve Trovato • **Private Lessons**
00695181 Book/CD Pack $16.99

Exotic Scales & Licks for Electric Guitar
by Jean Marc Belkadi • **Private Lessons**
00695860 Book/CD Pack $16.95

Funk Guitar
by Ross Bolton • **Private Lessons**
00695419 Book/CD Pack $15.99

Guitar Basics
by Bruce Buckingham • **Private Lessons**
00695134 Book/Online Audio $17.99

Guitar Fretboard Workbook
by Barrett Tagliarino • **Essential Concepts**
00695712 . . . . $19.99

Guitar Hanon
by Peter Deneff • **Private Lessons**
00695321 . . . . $14.99

Guitar Lick•tionary
by Dave Hill • **Private Lessons**
00695482 Book/CD Pack $21.99

Guitar Soloing
by Dan Gilbert & Beth Marlis • **Essential Concepts**
00695190 Book/CD Pack $22.99

Harmonics
by Jamie Findlay • **Private Lessons**
00695169 Book/CD Pack $13.99

Harmony & Theory
by Keith Wyatt & Carl Schroeder • **Essential Concepts**
00695169 . . . . $22.99

Introduction to Jazz Guitar Soloing
by Joe Elliott • **Master Class**
00695161 Book/Online Audio $19.95

Jazz Guitar Chord System
by Scott Henderson • **Private Lessons**
00695291 . . . . $12.99

Jazz Guitar Improvisation
by Sid Jacobs • **Master Class**
00217711 Book/Online Media $19.99

Jazz, Rock & Funk Guitar
by Dean Brown • **Private Lessons**
00217690 Book/Online Media $19.99

Jazz-Rock Triad Improvising
by Jean Marc Belkadi • **Private Lessons**
00695361 Book/CD Pack $15.99

Latin Guitar
by Bruce Buckingham • **Master Class**
00695379 Book/Online Audio $17.99

Lead Sheet Bible
by Robin Randall & Janice Peterson • **Private Lessons**
00695130 Book/CD Pack $22.99

Liquid Legato
by Allen Hinds • **Private Lessons**
00696656 Book/Online Audio $16.99

Modern Jazz Concepts for Guitar
by Sid Jacobs • **Master Class**
00695711 Book/CD Pack $16.95

Modern Rock Rhythm Guitar
by Danny Gill • **Private Lessons**
00695682 Book/Online Audio $19.99

Modes for Guitar
by Tom Kolb • **Private Lessons**
00695555 Book/Online Audio $18.99

Music Reading for Guitar
by David Oakes • **Essential Concepts**
00695192 . . . . $19.99

The Musician's Guide to Recording Acoustic Guitar
by Dallan Beck • **Master Class**
00695505 Book/CD Pack $13.99

Outside Guitar Licks
by Jean Marc Belkadi • **Private Lessons**
00695697 Book/CD Pack $16.99

Power Plucking
by Dale Turner • **Private Lesson**
00695962 Book/CD Pack $19.95

Progressive Tapping Licks
by Jean Marc Belkadi • **Private Lessons**
00695748 Book/CD Pack $17.99

Rhythm Guitar
by Bruce Buckingham & Eric Paschal • **Essential Concepts**
00695188 Book $19.99
00114559 Book/Online Audio $24.99
00695909 DVD $19.95

Rhythmic Lead Guitar
by Barrett Tagliarino • **Private Lessons**
00110263 Book/Online Audio $19.99

Rock Lead Basics
by Nick Nolan & Danny Gill • **Master Class**
00695144 Book/Online Audio $18.99
00695910 DVD $19.95

Rock Lead Performance
by Nick Nolan & Danny Gill • **Master Class**
00695278 Book/Online Audio $17.99

Rock Lead Techniques
by Nick Nolan & Danny Gill • **Master Class**
00695146 Book/Online Audio $16.99

Shred Guitar
by Greg Harrison • **Master Class**
00695977 Book/CD Pack $19.99

Slap & Pop Technique for Guitar
by Jean Marc Bekaldi • **Private Lessons**
00695645 Book/CD Pack $17.99

Solo Slap Guitar
by Jude Gold • **Master Class**
00139556 Book/Online Video $19.99

Technique Exercises for Guitar
by Jean Marc Belkadi • **Private Lessons**
00695913 Book/CD Pack $15.99

Texas Blues Guitar
by Robert Calva • **Private Lessons**
00695340 Book/Online Audio $17.99

Ultimate Guitar Technique
by Bill LaFleur • **Private Lessons**
00695863 Book/Online Audio $22.99

Prices, contents, and availability subject to change without notice.

7777 W. BLUEMOUND RD. P.O. BOX 13819 MILWAUKEE, WI 53213
www.halleonard.com

1120
031